# Living
# Signposts

© Copyright Mrs A. Steele
December 1999

## JANUARY

### The Storm

*The night sky hangs forebodingly*
*With storm clouds in a swirl,*
*Yet though our ship is tempest tossed,*
*God's people fear no ill.*

*The waves rise up, like rolling hills*
*Above our heads they tower,*
*But Jesus is the captain's name,*
*He keeps us by His power.*

*Believer, trust in Christ the Lord*
*Though waves beat on your face,*
*For all the struggles of this life*
*Will help you grow in grace.*

*Endure my friend, for soon we'll see*
*The light beyond the storm,*
*The light that shines for ever more,*
*A harbour safe, in heaven.*

## JANUARY — *Long-suffering*

**15th** Despisest thou the riches of His goodness and forbearance and long-suffering?

*Rom. 2:4*

**16th** Long-suffering to us-ward, not willing that any should perish, but that all should come to repentance.

*2 Peter 3:9*

**17th** Thou, O Lord, art a God full of compassion, and gracious, long-suffering.

*Ps. 86:15*

**18th** Put on therefore, as the elect of God ... kindness, humbleness of mind, meekness, long-suffering.

*Col. 3:12*

**19th** Forbearing one another, and forgiving one another, if any man have a quarrel against any.

*Col. 3:13*

**20th** The fruit of the Spirit is love, joy, peace, long-suffering.

*Gal 5:22*

**21st** Strengthened with all might, according to His glorious power, unto all patience and long-suffering with joyfulness.

*Col. 1:11*

## JANUARY — *Happiness*

**22nd** Blessed is every one that feareth the Lord; that walketh in His ways ... Happy shalt thou be.
*Ps. 128:1-2*

**23rd** Be glad in the Lord, and rejoice, ye righteous: and shout for joy, all ye that are upright in heart.
*Ps. 32:11*

**24th** If ye suffer for righteousness' sake, happy are ye: and be not afraid.
*I Peter 3:14*

**25th** If ye be reproached for the name of Christ, happy are ye.
*I Peter 4:14.*

**26th** The Lord hath done great things for us; whereof we are glad.
*Ps. 126:3*

**27th** Happy is the man that findeth wisdom, and the man that getteth understanding.
*Prov. 3:13*

**28th** In Thy presence is fulness of joy; at Thy right hand there are pleasures for evermore.
*Ps. 16:11.*

**29th** Whoso trusteth in the Lord, happy is he.
*Prov. 16:20*

**30th** Happy is that people, whose God is the Lord.
*Ps. 144:15*

**31st** If ye know these things, happy are ye if ye do them.
*John 13:17*

## FEBRUARY

### *Ebenezer*

*Not one single moment passes,*
*But is laden, as it flies,*
*With some precious gift of blessing,*
*Which His loving care supplies.*

*Not one step, in faith, is taken,*
*O'er life's pathway rough and dim,*
*But may open out new treasures*
*To the soul that trusts in Him.*

*Ebenezer! countless mercies,*
*Bid us praise Him more and more,*
*Calmly to His wisdom leaving*
*What the future has in store.*

*Let no faithless thought, arising,*
*Hide His presence from our view,*
*He will nevermore forsake us,*
*Who hath blessed us hitherto.*

B.H.

## FEBRUARY — *Courage*

**1st** Be strong and of a good courage ... for the Lord thy God is with thee whithersoever thou goest.
*Joshua 1:9*

**2nd** We have no might against this great company that cometh against us ... but our eyes are upon Thee.
*2 Chron 20:12*

**3rd** We may boldly say, The Lord is my helper, and I will not fear what man shall do unto me.
*Heb. 13:6*

**4th** Shadrach, Meshach, and Abednego, answered ... we are not careful to answer thee in this matter.
*Daniel 3:16*

**5th** Arise; for this matter belongeth unto thee: we also will be with thee: be of good courage, and do it.
*Ezra 10:4.*

**6th** Grant unto Thy servants, that with all boldness they may speak Thy word.
*Acts 4:29*

**7th** They were all filled with the Holy Ghost, and they spake the word of God with boldness.
*Acts 4:31*

## ☙ FEBRUARY ❧ — *Adversity*

**8th** They cried unto the Lord in their trouble, and He delivered them out of their distresses.

*Ps. 107:6*

**9th** Ye have this day rejected the Lord your God, Who Himself saved you out of all your adversities.

*1 Sam. 10:19*

**10th** If thou faint in the day of adversity, thy strength is small.

*Prov. 24:10*

**11th** He shall call upon Me, and I will answer him: I will be with him in trouble.

*Ps. 91:15*

**12th** I poured out my complaint before Him; I shewed before His my trouble.

*Ps. 142:2*

**13th** Thou hast considered my trouble; Thou hast known my soul in adversities.

*Ps. 31:7*

**14th** When thou passest through the waters, I will be with thee.

*Isa. 43:2*

## ❧ FEBRUARY ❧ — *Confidence*

**15th** Being confident of this very thing, that He which hath begun a good work in you will perform it.
*Phil. 1:6*

**16th** Being fully persuaded that, what He had promised, He was able also to perform.
*Rom. 4:21*

**17th** Wherefore, sirs, be of good cheer: for I believe God, that it shall be even as it was told me.
*Acts 27:25*

**18th** My soul, wait thou only upon God; for my expectation is from Him.
*Ps. 62:5*

**19th** Blessed is she that believed: for there shall be a performance of those things which were told her.
*Luke 1:45*

**20th** Knowing in yourselves that ye have in heaven a better and an enduring substance.
*Heb. 10:34*

**21st** Cast not away therefore your confidence, which hath great recompense of reward.
*Heb. 10:35*

## FEBRUARY — *Glory*

**22nd** That we should be to the praise of His glory, who first trusted in Christ.

*Eph. 1:12*

**23rd** We all, with open face beholding as in a glass the glory of the Lord.

*2 Cor. 3:18*

**24th** Changed into the same image from glory to glory.
*2 Cor. 3:18*

**25th** The Spirit of glory and of God resteth upon you.
*1 Pet. 4:14*

**26th** Called ... to glory and virtue.

*2 Pet. 1:3*

**27th** Our light affliction ... worketh for us a far more exceeding and eternal weight of glory.

*2 Cor. 4:17*

**28th** I will make the place of My feet glorious.

*Isa. 60:13*

**29th** The glory which Thou gavest Me. I have given them.
*John 17:22*

# MARCH

## Lend A Hand

*If any little word of mine*
*May make a life the brighter,*
*If any little song of mine*
*May make a heart the lighter -*

*God help me speak the little word,*
*And take my bit of singing,*
*And drop it in some lonely vale*
*To set the echoes ringing.*

*If any little love of mine*
*May make a life the sweeter,*
*If any little care of mine*
*May make a friend's the fleeter.*

*If any lift of mine may ease*
*The burden of another -*
*God give me love, and care, and strength*
*To help my toiling brother.*

## ❦ MARCH ❦  *Kindness*

**1ˢᵗ** Be ye kind one to another, tenderhearted, forgiving one another.

*Eph. 4:32*

**2ⁿᵈ** Bear ye one another's burdens, and so fulfil the law of Christ.

*Gal. 6:2*

**3ʳᵈ** The Lord deal kindly with you, as ye have dealt … with me.

*Ruth 1:8*

**4ᵗʰ** He had compassion on him, and went to him, and bound up his wounds.

*Luke 10:33-34*

**5ᵗʰ** And set him on his own beast, and brought him to an inn, and took care of him.

*Luke 10:34*

**6ᵗʰ** Take care of him; and whatsoever thou spendest more, when I come again, I will repay thee.

*Luke 10:35*

**7ᵗʰ** Inasmuch as ye have done it unto one of the least of these … ye have done it unto Me.

*Matt. 25:40*

## ❧ MARCH ❧  *Sincerity*

**8th** The Lord seeth not as man seeth ... on the outward appearance, but the Lord looketh on the heart.
*I Sam. 16:7*

**9th** Fear the Lord, and serve Him in sincerity and in truth.
*Joshua 24:14*

**10th** The Lord searcheth all hearts, and understandeth all the imaginations of the thoughts.
*I Chron. 28:9*

**11th** Grace be with all them that love our Lord Jesus Christ in sincerity.
*Eph. 6:24*

**12th** Search me, O God, and know my heart: try me, and know my thoughts.
*Ps. 139:23*

**13th** And this I pray ... that ye may be sincere and without offence till the day of Christ.
*Phil 1:9-10*

**14th** In all things shewing thyself a pattern of good works: in doctrine shewing uncorruptness, gravity, sincerity.
*Titus 2:7*

## MARCH — *Suffering*

**15th** Unto you it is given in the behalf of Christ, not only to believe on Him, but also to suffer for His sake.
*Phil. 1:29*

**16th** These three men ... fell down bound into the midst of the burning fiery furnace.
*Daniel 3:23*

**17th** When thou walkest through the fire, thou shalt not be burned.
*Isa. 43:2*

**18th** Four men loose, walking in the midst of the fire, and they have no hurt.
*Daniel 3:25*

**19th** The form of the fourth is like the Son of God. God Whom we serve is able to deliver us.
*Daniel 3:25, 17*

**20th** Let them that suffer according to the will of God commit the keeping of their souls to Him.
*1 Peter 4:19*

**21st** Fear none of those things which thou shalt suffer.
*Rev. 2:10*

# ❧ MARCH ❧ *Support*

**22nd** Yea, they spake against God; they said, Can God furnish a table in the wilderness?

*Ps. 78:19*

**23rd** Thou ... withheldest not Thy manna from their mouth, and gavest them water for their thirst.

*Neh. 9:20*

**24th** Yea, forty years didst Thou sustain them in the wilderness so that they lacked nothing.

*Neh. 9:21*

**25th** Thou preparest a table before me in the presence of mine enemies ... my cup runneth over.

*Ps. 23:5*

**26th** It shall be, that thou shalt drink of the brook; and I have commanded the ravens to feed thee there.

*1 Kings 17:4*

**27th** The barrel of meal wasted not, neither did the cruse of oil fail, according to the word of the Lord.

*1 Kings 17:16*

**28th** Blessed shall be thy basket and thy store.

*Deut. 28:5*

**29th** Trust in the Lord and do good, so shalt thou dwell in the land, and verily thou shalt be fed.

*Ps. 37:3*

**30th** Your Father knoweth that ye have need of these things.

*Luke 12:30*

**31st** But rather seek ye the kingdom of God; and all these things shall be added unto you.

*Luke 12:31*

## APRIL

## Trust

*If thou but suffer God to guide thee,*
*And hope in Him through all thy ways,*
*He'll give thee strength whate'er betide thee,*
*And bear thee through the evil days;*
*Who trusts in God's unchanging love*
*Builds on the rock that nought can move.*

*Only be still, and wait His leisure*
*In cheerful hope, with heart content*
*To take whate'er thy Father's pleasure*
*And all-discerning love have sent;*
*Nor doubt our inmost wants are known*
*To Him who chose us for His own.*

*Sing, pray, and keep His ways unswerving;*
*So do thine own part faithfully,*
*And trust His word - though undeserving,*
*Thou yet shalt find it true for thee:*
*God never yet forsook at need*
*The soul that trusted Him indeed.*

## APRIL — *Quietness*

**1st** Study to be quiet, and to do your own business and to work with your own hands.

*1 Thess. 4:11*

**2nd** We should live soberly, righteously, and godly, in this present world.

*Titus 2:12*

**3rd** The ornament of a meek and quiet spirit, which is in the sight of God of great price.

*1 Pet. 3:4*

**4th** In quietness and in confidence shall be your strength.

*Isa. 30:15*

**5th** When He giveth quietness who then can make trouble?

*Job 34:29*

**6th** The work of righteousness shall be peace; and the effect … quietness and assurance for ever.

*Isa. 32:17*

**7th** The peace of God, which passeth all understanding, shall keep your hearts and minds through Christ Jesus.

*Phil 4:7*

## ❧ APRIL ❧ *The Way*

**8th** There is a way which seemeth right unto a man, but the end thereof are the ways of death.
*Prov. 14:12*

**9th** Enter ye in at the strait gate ... strait is the gate, and narrow is the way, which leadeth unto life.
*Matt. 7:13-14.*

**10th** He knoweth the way that I take: when He hath tried me, I shall come forth as gold.
*Job 23:10*

**11th** Commit thy way unto the Lord; trust also in Him; and He shall bring it to pass.
*Ps. 37:5*

**12th** In all thy ways acknowledge Him, and He shall direct thy paths.
*Prov. 3:6.*

**13th** I am the Resurrection, and the Life: he that believeth in Me, though he were dead, yet shall he live.
*John 11:25*

**14th** He led them forth by the right way, that they might go to a city of habitation.
*Ps. 107:7*

## ⁂ APRIL ⁂

**15th** The Eternal God is thy refuge, and underneath are the everlasting arms.
*Deut. 33:27*

**16th** My soul trusteth in Thee: yea in the shadow of Thy wings will I make my refuge.
*Ps. 57:1*

**17th** Thou shalt call His name JESUS: for He shall save His people from their sins.
*Matt. 1:21*

**18th** There is none other name under heaven given among men, whereby, we must be saved.
*Acts 4:12*

**19th** The name of the Lord is a strong tower: the righteous runneth into it, and is safe.
*Prov. 18:10.*

**20th** Refuge failed me; no man cared for my soul. I cried unto THEE … I said, Thou art my refuge.
*Ps. 142:4-5*

**21st** I will sing aloud of Thy mercy in the morning: for Thou hast been my defence and refuge in the day of my trouble.
*Ps. 59:16*

## APRIL — *Comfort*

**22ⁿᵈ** If I be lifted up from the earth, will draw all men unto Me.

*John 12:32*

**23ʳᵈ** The God of all comfort; Who comforteth us in all our tribulation.

*2 Cor. 1:3-4*

**24ᵗʰ** In the multitude of my thoughts within me Thy comforts delight my soul.

*Ps. 94:19*

**25ᵗʰ** We through patience and comfort of the Scriptures might have hope.

*Rom. 15:4*

**26ᵗʰ** I remembered Thy judgments of old, O Lord; and have comforted myself.

*Ps. 119:52*

**27ᵗʰ** Comfort them which are in any trouble by the comfort wherewith we ourselves are comforted of God.

*2 Cor. 1:4*

**28ᵗʰ** So shall we ever be with the Lord. Wherefore comfort one another with these words.

*1 Thess. 4:17-18*

**29ᵗʰ** As the sufferings of Christ abound in us, so our consolation also aboundeth by Christ.

*2 Cor. 1:5*

**30ᵗʰ** If we suffer; we shall also reign with Him.

*2 Tim. 2:12*

## MAY

### He Is Able

*Fierce and dread the tempest gathers,*
*Dark clouds drift across our sky,*
*All around suspense and tumult,*
*Waves of trouble rising high.*
*But our trust is in Jehovah,*
*Who the wildest storm canst still;*
*God has promised to deliver -*
*He is able, and He will!*

*Day by day fresh suff'ring threatens,*
*Anxious thoughts of peril near,*
*Grief and pain of separation.*
*Loss of all we hold most dear.*
*Yet amidst the sharpest anguish*
*Perfect peace our hearts can fill;*
*God has promised to deliver -*
*He is able, and He will.*

S.B. Kathleen Warren

## ❧ MAY ❧ — *Consolation*

**1st** We ... have a strong consolation, who have fled for refuge to lay hold upon the hope set before us.
*Heb. 6:18*

**2nd** The sufferings of this present time are not worthy to be compared with the glory which shall be revealed in us.
*Rom. 8:18*

**3rd** If so be that we suffer with Him, that we may be also glorified together.
*Rom. 8:17*

**4th** Weeping may endure for a night, but joy cometh in the morning.
*Ps. 30:5*

**5th** Father, I will that they also whom Thou hast given Me, be with Me where I am.
*John 17:24.*

**6th** Eye hath not seen, nor ear heard ... the things which God hath prepared for them that love Him.
*1 Cor. 2:9*

**7th** As the sufferings of Christ abound in us, so our consolation also aboundeth by Christ.
*2 Cor. 1:5*

## ⌘ MAY ⌘  *Praise*

---

**8th**  Bless the Lord, O my soul: and all that is within me, bless His holy mane.

*Ps. 103:1*

**9th**  What shall I render unto the Lord for all His benefits toward me?

*Ps. 116:12*

**10th**  Go home to thy friends, and tell them how great things the Lord hath done for thee.

*Mark 5:19*

**11th**  He hath put a new song in my mouth, even praise unto our God.

*Ps. 40:3*

**12th**  While I live will I praise the Lord: I will sing praises unto my God while I have any being.

*Ps. 146:2*

**13th**  The praises of Him Who hath called you out of darkness into His marvellous light.

*1 Peter 2:9*

**14th**  I heard the voice of harpers harping with their harps: and they sung as it were a new song before the throne.

*Rev. 14:2-3*

## MAY — *Deliverance*

**15th** Ye shall not need to fight in this battle: set yourselves, stand ye still, and see the salvation of the Lord.
*2 Chron. 20:7*

**16h** Call upon Me in the day of trouble: I will deliver thee, and thou shalt glorify Me.
*Ps. 50:15*

**17th** My God hath sent His angel and hath shut the lions' mouths, that they have not hurt me.
*Daniel 6:22*

**18th** The weapons of our warfare are not carnal, but mighty through God to the pulling down of strong holds.
*2 Cor. 10:4*

**19th** Casting down imaginations, and every high things that exalteth itself against the knowledge of God.
*2 Cor. 10:5*

**20th** (Jesus) laid His hands on her: and immediately she was made straight, and glorified God.
*Luke 13:13*

**21st** (God) hath delivered us from the power of darkness, and hath translated us into the kingdom of His dear son.
*Col. 1:13*

## MAY — *Prosperity*

**22**[th] The Lord was with (Hezekiah); and he prospered whithersoever he went.
*2 Kings 18:7*

**23**[th] The Lord was with (Joseph), and that which he did, the Lord made it to prosper.
*Gen. 39:23*

**24**[th] Let the Lord be magnified, which hath pleasure in the prosperity of his servant.
*Ps. 35:27*

**25**[th] As long as (Uzziah) sought the Lord, God made him to prosper.
*2 Chron. 26:5.*

**26**[th] Who hath hardened himself against Him, and hath prospered?
*Job 9:4*

**27**[th] Prosper, I pray Thee, Thy servant this day.
*Neh. 1:11*

**28**[h] The God of heaven, He will prosper us; therefore we His servants will arise and build.
*Neh. 2:20*

**29**[th] Establish Thou the work of our hands upon us.
*Ps. 90:17*

**30**[th] Riches and honour are with Me, yea, durable riches and righteousness.
*Prov. 8:18*

**31**[th] This book of the law shall not depart out of thy mouth, but thou shalt meditate therein day and night that thou mayest observe to do all that is written therein, for then shalt thou make thy way prosperous, and then thou shalt have good success.
*Josh. 1:8*

# JUNE

## The Bright Side

*If we noticed little pleasures
As we notice little pains;
If we quite forgot our losses
And remembered all our gains;
If we looked for people's virtues,
And their faults refused to see,
What a comfortable, happy,
Cheerful place this world would be!*

## JUNE — *Riches*

**1st** Let not the rich man glory in his riches.
*Jer. 9:23*

**2nd** Labour not to be rich ... Riches certainly make themselves wings.
*Prov. 23:4-5*

**3rd** Charge them that are rich in this world ... that they be rich in good works.
*1 Tim. 6:17-18*

**4th** There is that maketh himself rich, yet hath nothing: there is that maketh himself poor, yet hath great riches.
*Prov. 13:7*

**5th** I know thy works, and tribulation, and poverty (but thou art rich).
*Rev. 2:9*

**6th** As poor, yet making many rich; as having nothing, and yet possessing all things.
*2 Cor. 6:10*

**7th** I counsel thee to buy of Me gold tried in the fire, that thou mayest be rich.
*Rev. 3:18*

## JUNE — Rest

**8th** Come unto Me, all ye that labour and are heavy laden, and I will give you rest.

*Matt. 11:28*

**9th** Learn of Me; for I am meek and lowly in heart: and ye shall find rest unto your souls.

*Matt. 11:29*

**10th** My Presence shall go with thee, and I will give thee rest.

*Exodus 33:14*

**11th** He maketh me to lie down in green pastures: He leadeth me beside the still waters.

*Ps. 23:2*

**12th** My people shall dwell in a peaceable habitation, and in sure dwellings, and in quiet resting places.

*Isa. 32:18*

**13th** In My Father's house are many mansions: if it were not so, I would have told you. I go to prepare a place for you.

*John 14:2*

**14th** Rest in the Lord, and wait patiently for Him.

*Ps. 37:7*

## ⊰ JUNE ⊱  *Chastisement*

**15th** My son, despise not the chastening of the Lord; neither be weary of His correction.
*Prov. 3:11*

**16th** Whom the Lord loveth He chasteneth, and scourgeth every son whom He receiveth.
*Heb. 12:6*

**17th** Chastening ... yieldeth the peaceable fruit of righteousness unto them which are exercised thereby.
*Heb. 12:11*

**18th** He shall pray unto God, and He will be favourable unto him: and he shall see His face with joy.
*Job. 33:26*

**19th** Lord, be merciful unto me: heal my soul; for I have sinned against Thee.
*Ps. 41:4*

**20th** Surely it is meet to be said unto God, I have borne chastisement, I will not offend any more.
*Job. 34:31*

**21st** Now mine eye seeth Thee. Wherefore I abhor myself, and repent in dust and ashes.
*Job: 42:5-6*

## JUNE — *Treasures*

**22nd** The Lord shall open unto thee His good treasure.
*Deut. 28:12*

**23rd** God so loved the world, that He gave his only begotten Son.
*John 3:16*

**24th** How shall He not with Him also freely give us all things?
*Rom. 8:32*

**25th** Seek those things which are above, where Christ sitteth on the right hand of God.
*Col. 3:1*

**26th** Lay not up for yourselves treasures upon earth ... but lay up for yourselves treasures in heaven.
*Matt. 6:19-20*

**27th** Provide yourselves bags which wax not old, a treasure in the heavens that faileth not.
*Luke 12:33*

**28th** For where your treasure is, there will your heart be also.
*Luke 12:34*

**29th** I will give thee the treasures of darkness.
*Isa. 45:3*

**30th** The kingdom of heaven is like unto treasure hid in a field, the which when a man hath found, he hideth, and for joy thereof goeth and selleth all that he hath and buyeth that field.
*Matt. 13:44*

# JULY

## Communion

*Begin the day with God;*
*Kneel down to Him in prayer;*
*Lift up thy heart to His abode,*
*And seek His love to share.*

*Open the Book of God,*
*And read a portion there,*
*That it may hallow all thy thoughts,*
*And sweeten all thy care.*

*Go through the day with God,*
*Whate'er thy work may be;*
*Where'er thou art - at home, abroad,*
*He is still near to thee.*

*Lie down at night with God,*
*Who gives His servants sleep;*
*And when thou tread'st the vale of death*
*He will thee guard and keep.*

## JULY — *Works*

**1st** God is not unrighteous to forget your work and labour of love, which ye have shewed toward His Name.
*Heb. 6:10*

**2nd** Joanna ... and Susanna, and many others, which ministered unto Him of their substance.
*Luke 8:3*

**3rd** There came unto Him a woman having an alabaster box of very precious ointment, and poured it on His head.
*Matt. 26:7*

**4th** Your work of faith, and labour of love, and patience of hope in our Lord Jesus Christ.
*1 Thess. 1:3*

**5th** Whosoever shall give you a cup of water to drink in My name, because ye belong to Christ ... he shall not lose his reward.
*Mark 9:41*

**6th** I was an hungered, and ye gave Me meat: I was thirsty, and ye gave Me drink.
*Matt. 25:35*

**7th** Behold, I come quickly; and My reward is with Me, to give every man according as his work shall be.
*Rev. 22:12*

# JULY — *Loyalty*

**8th** It is required in stewards, that a man be found faithful.

*1 Cor. 4:2*

**9th** As every man hath received the gift, even so minister the same one to another, as good stewards.

*1 Peter 4:10*

**10th** His servants ... yielded their bodies that they might not serve nor worship any god, except their own God.

*Daniel 3:28*

**11th** No man can serve two masters ... Ye cannot serve God and mammon.

*Matt 6:24*

**12th** Whether it be right in the sight of God to hearken unto you more than unto God, judge ye.

*Acts 4:19*

**13th** Study to shew thyself approved unto God, a workman that needeth not to be ashamed.

*2 Tim. 2:15*

**14th** Well done, thou good and faithful servant:... enter thou into the joy of thy Lord.

*Matt. 25:21*

## JULY — *Guidance*

**15th** I will instruct thee and teach thee in the way which thou shalt go: I will guide thee with Mine eye.

*Ps. 32:8*

**16th** The Lord shall guide thee continually, and satisfy thy soul in drought.

*Isa. 58:11*

**17th** He knoweth thy walking through this great wilderness ... thou hast lacked nothing.

*Deut. 2:7*

**18th** When He putteth forth His own sheep, He goeth before them, and the sheep follow Him.

*John 10:4*

**19th** He that hath mercy on them shall lead them, even by the springs of water shall He guide them.

*Isa. 49:10*

**20th** Thou shalt guide me with Thy counsel, and afterward receive me to glory.

*Ps. 73:24*

**21st** The Lamb ... shall lead them unto living fountains of waters: and God shall wipe away all tears from their eyes.

*Rev. 7:17*

## JULY — *Submission*

**22nd** Let us behave ourselves valiantly ... and let the Lord do that which is good in His sight.
*1 Chron. 19:13*

**23rd** Though He slay me, yet will I trust in Him.
*Job 13:15*

**24th** The Lord gave, and the Lord hath taken away; blessed be the name of the Lord.
*Job 1:21*

**25th** Submit yourselves therefore to God. Resist the devil, and he will flee from you.
*James 4:7*

**26th** It is the Lord: let Him do what seemeth Him good.
*1 Sam. 3:18*

**27th** Though He cause grief, yet will He have compassion according to the multitude of His mercies.
*Lam. 3:32*

**28th** Working in you that which is well-pleasing in His sight.
*Heb. 13:21*

**29th** He knoweth the way that I take; when He hath tried me I shall come forth as gold.
*Job 23:10*

**30th** He shall sit as a refiner and purifier of silver.
*Mal. 3:3*

**31st** Humble yourselves therefore under the mighty hand of God, that He may exalt you in due time.
*1 Pet. 5:6*

## AUGUST

### *Better To Hope*

'Tis better to hope, though the clouds hang low,
    And to keep the eyes uplifted;
For the bright blue sky will soon peep through
    When the ominous clouds are rifted.
There was never a night without a day
    Or an evening without a morning;
And the darkest hour, as the proverb says,
    Is the hour before the dawning.

Seek, then, to weave in the web of life
    A bright and a golden filling,
And to do God's will with a gladsome heart
    And hands that are ready and willing;
For the sunny soul that is full of hope,
    And whose trust in God ne'er faileth,
Knows "God is love" and "God is light,"
    Though at times the storm prevaileth.

                              Selected.

# AUGUST — *Hope*

**1st** Rejoicing in hope; patient in tribulation; continuing instant in prayer.
*Rom. 12:12*

**2nd** Why art thou cast down, O my soul? and why art thou disquieted within me? hope thou in God.
*Ps. 42:11*

**3rd** It is good that a man should both hope and quietly wait for the salvation of the Lord.
*Lam. 3:26*

**4th** (Abraham) against hope believed in hope.
*Rom. 4:18*

**5th** Blessed is the man that trusteth in the Lord, and whose hope the Lord is.
*Jer. 17:7*

**6th** Be sober, and hope to the end for the grace that is to be brought unto you.
*1 Peter 1:13*

**7th** Looking for that blessed hope, and the glorious appearing of the Great God and our Saviour Jesus Christ.
*Titus 2:13*

# AUGUST — *Redemption*

**8th** Christ hath redeemed us from the curse of the law, being made a curse for us.

*Gal. 3:13*

**9th** Thou wast slain, and hast redeemed us to God by Thy blood out of every kindred, and tongue, and people, and nation.

*Rev. 5:9*

**10th** They which live should not henceforth live unto themselves, but unto Him which died for them, and rose again.

*2 Cor. 5:15*

**11th** I know that my Redeemer liveth, and that He shall stand at the latter day upon the earth.

*Job 19:25*

**12th** We ourselves groan within ourselves, waiting for the adoption, to wit, the redemption of our body.

*Rom. 8:23*

**13th** We shall not all sleep, but we shall all be changed, in a moment, in the twinkling of an eye.

*1 Cor 15:51-52*

**14h** Unto Him that loved us, and washed us from our sins in His own blood … to Him be glory.

*Rev. 1:5-6*

# ❧ AUGUST ❧　　　　　　　　　　　*Peace*

**15th** Being justified by faith, we have peace with God through our Lord Jesus Christ.

*Rom. 5:1*

**16th** Peace I leave with you, My peace I give unto you … Let not your heart be troubled, neither let it be afraid.

*John 14:27*

**17th** Thou wilt keep him in perfect peace, whose mind is stayed on Thee: because he trusted in Thee.

*Isa. 26:3*

**18th** To be carnally minded is death; but to be spiritually minded is life and peace.

*Rom. 8:6*

**19th** Ye shall go out with joy, and be led forth with peace.

*Isa. 55:12*

**20th** The peace of God, which passeth all understanding, shall keep your hearts and minds through Christ Jesus.

*Phil. 4:7*

**21st** The Lord of peace Himself give you peace always by all means.

*2 Thess. 3:16*

# ⚜ AUGUST ⚜ — *Love*

**22nd** God commendeth His love toward us, in that, while we were yet sinners, Christ died for us.
*Rom. 5:8*

**23rd** We have known and believed the love that God hath to us. God is love.
*1 John 4:16*

**24th** Beloved, if God so loved us, we ought also to love one another.
*1 John 4:11*

**25th** This is His commandment, That we should believe on the Name of His Son ... and love one another.
*1 John 3:23*

**26th** He that hath My commandments, and keepeth them, he it is that loveth Me.
*John 14:21*

**27th** Ye yourselves are taught of God to love one another.
*1 Thess. 4:9*

**28th** Walk in Love as Christ also hath loved us.
*Eph. 5:2*

**29th** He that loveth Me shall be loved of My Father, and I will love him, and will manifest Myself to him.
*John 14: 21*

**30th** That ye, being rooted and grounded in love, may be able to comprehend ... and to know the love of Christ which passeth knowledge.
*Eph. 3:17-19*

**31st** Love as brethren, be pitiful, be courteous.
*1 Pet. 3:8*

## SEPTEMBER

### Just Being Happy

*Just being happy
Is a fine thing to do;
Looking on the bright side
Rather than the blue;
Sad or sunny musing
Is largely in the choosing,
And just being happy
Is brave work and true.*

*Just being happy
Helps other souls along;
Their burdens may be heavy,
And they not strong;
And your own sky will lighten
If other skies you brighten
By just being happy
With a heart full of song!*

Selected

## SEPTEMBER

*Joy*

**1st**    The joy of the Lord is your strength.
*Neh. 8:10*

**2nd**    In whom, though now ye see Him not, yet believing, ye rejoice with joy unspeakable and full of glory.
*1 Peter 1:8*

**3rd**    I will greatly rejoice in the Lord, my soul shall be joyful in my God.
*Isa. 61:10*

**4th**    I am filled with comfort, I am exceeding joyful in all our tribulation.
*2 Cor. 7:4*

**5th**    Looking unto Jesus … Who for the joy that was set before Him endured the cross, despising the shame.
*Heb 12:2*

**6th**    Rejoice, inasmuch as ye are partakers of Christ's sufferings.
*1 Peter 4:13*

**7th**    That, when His glory shall be revealed, ye may be glad also with exceeding joy.
*1 Peter 4:13*

## ☙ SEPTEMBER ❧              *Gentleness*

---

***8th***   The fruit of the Spirit is … gentleness.

*Gal. 5:22*

***9th***   The servant of the Lord must not strive; but be gentle.

*2 Tim. 2:24*

***10th***   Gentle, shewing all meekness unto all men.

*Titus 3:2*

***11th***   Not rendering evil for evil, or railing for railing: but contrariwise blessing.

*1 Peter 3:9*

***12th***   The wisdom that is from above is first pure, then peaceable, gentle.

*James 3:17*

***13th***   (Jesus) when He was reviled, reviled not again; when He suffered, He threatened not.

*1 Peter 2:23*

***14th***   A soft answer turneth away wrath: but grievous words stir up anger.

*Prov. 15:1*

## SEPTEMBER — *Righteousness*

**15th** He hath clothed me with the garments of salvation, He hath covered me with the robe of righteousness.
*Isa. 61:10*

**16th** Even the righteousness of God which is by faith of Jesus Christ
*Rom. 3:22*

**17th** Our old man is crucified with Him ... that henceforth we should not serve sin.
*Rom. 6:6*

**18th** Even so now yield your members servants to righteousness until holiness.
*Rom. 6:19*

**19th** What fellowship hath righteousness with unrighteousness? and what communion hath light with darkness?
*2 Cor. 6:14*

**20th** Present your bodies a living sacrifice, holy, acceptable unto God, which is your reasonable service.
*Rom. 12:1*

**21st** Filled with the fruits of righteousness, which are by Jesus Christ, unto the glory and praise of God.
*Phil. 1:11*

## ❧ SEPTEMBER ❧           *Faith*

**22<sup>nd</sup>** Without faith it is impossible to please Him.

*Heb. 11:6*

**23<sup>rd</sup>** Being justified by faith, we have peace with God through our Lord Jesus Christ.

*Rom. 5:1*

**24<sup>th</sup>** The life which I now live in the flesh I live by the faith of the Son of God, Who loved me.

*Gal. 2:20*

**25<sup>th</sup>** Who is he that overcometh the world, but he that believeth that Jesus is the Son of God?

*1 John 5:5*

**26<sup>th</sup>** By faith Abraham, when he was called to go out ... obeyed; and he went out, not knowing whither he went.

*Heb. 11:8*

**27<sup>th</sup>** He staggered not at the promise of God through unbelief; but was strong in faith.

*Rom. 4:20*

**28<sup>th</sup>** The trial of your faith, being much more precious than of gold that perisheth.

*1 Peter 1:7*

**29<sup>th</sup>** We walk by faith not by sight.

*2 Cor. 5:7*

**30<sup>th</sup>** Lord, increase our faith.

*Luke 17:5*

# OCTOBER

## Tender And True

*Just to be tender, just to be true;*
*Just to be glad the whole day through;*
*Just to be merciful, just to be mild;*
*Just to be trustful as a child;*
*Just to be gentle and kind and sweet;*
*Just to be helpful with willing feet;*
*Just to be cheery when things go wrong,*
*Just to drive sadness away with song;*
*Whether the hour is dark or bright,*
*Just to be loyal to God and the right;*
*Just to believe that God knows best;*
*Just in His promises ever to rest;*
*Just to let love be our daily key -*
*This is God's will for you and me*

Selected.

# OCTOBER — *Steadfastness*

**1st**    He is the living God, and steadfast for ever.
*Dan. 6:26*

**2nd**    Beware lest ye also, being led away with the error of the wicked, fall from your own steadfastness.
*2 Peter 3:17*

**3rd**    The devil ... walketh about seeking whom he may devour: whom resist steadfast in the faith.
*1 Peter 5:8-9*

**4th**    Ye have not yet resisted unto blood, striving against sin.
*Heb. 12:4*

**5th**    Be ye steadfast, unmoveable, always abounding in the work of the Lord.
*1 Cor. 15:58*

**6th**    Rooted and built up in Him, and stablished in the faith ... abounding therein with thanksgiving.
*Col. 2:7*

**7th**    Let us not be weary in well doing: for in due season we shall reap, if we faint not.
*Gal. 6:9*

## ❈ OCTOBER ❈ *Humility*

**8th**  Before destruction the heart of man is haughty, and before honour is humility.
*Prov. 18:12*

**9th**  Humble yourselves in the sight of the Lord, and He shall lift you up.
*James 4:10*

**10th**  Every one that is proud in heart is an abomination to the Lord ... he shall not be unpunished.
*Prov. 16:5*

**11th**  The publican standing afar off ... smote upon his breast, saying, God be merciful to me a sinner.
*Luke 18:13*

**12th**  Every one that exalteth himself shall be abased; and he that humbleth himself shall be exalted.
*Luke 18:14*

**13th** Humble yourselves therefore under the mighty hand of God that He may exalt you in due time.
*1 Peter 5:6*

**14th**  I dwell in the high and holy places, with him also that is of a contrite and humble spirit.
*Isa. 57:15*

## ❧ OCTOBER ❧ — *Access*

**15th** I am the Way, the Truth, and the Life: no man cometh unto the Father, but by Me.

*John 14:6*

**16th** We have boldness and access with confidence by the faith of Him.

*Eph 3:12*

**17th** The king held out the golden sceptre toward Esther. So Esther arose, and stood before the king.

*Esther 8:4*

**18th** Let us therefore come boldly unto the throne of grace.

*Heb. 4:16*

**19th** Christ also hath once suffered ... that He might bring us to God.

*1 Peter 3:18*

**20th** By Whom also we have access by faith into this grace wherein we stand.

*Rom. 5:2*

**21st** Let us draw near with a true heart in full assurance of faith.

*Heb. 10:22*

## ◆ OCTOBER ◆ *Security*

**22ⁿᵈ** I give unto (My sheep) eternal life; and they shall never perish, neither shall any man pluck them out of My hand.

*John 10:28*

**23ʳᵈ** I know Whom I have believed, and am persuaded that He is able to keep that which I have committed unto Him.

*2 Tim 1:12*

**24ᵗʰ** Ye are the children of God by faith in Christ Jesus.

*Gal. 3:26*

**25ᵗʰ** If children, then heirs; heirs of God, and joint-heirs with Christ.

*Rom. 8:17*

**26ᵗʰ** Who shall lay anything to the charge of God's elect? It is God that justifieth.

*Rom. 8:33*

**27ᵗʰ** There is therefore now no condemnation to them which are in Christ Jesus.

*Rom. 8:1*

**28ᵗʰ** What shall we then say to these things? If God be for us, who can be against us?

*Rom. 8:31*

## OCTOBER — *Holiness*

**29**[th]  What manner of persons ought ye to be in all holy conversation and godliness?

*2 Peter 3:11*

**30**[th]  Put on the new man, which after God is created in righteousness and true holiness.

*Eph 4:24*

**31**[st]  Ye were sometimes darkness, but now are ye light in the Lord; walk as children of light.

*Eph. 5:8*

## NOVEMBER

### *Answers*

*I asked the Lord that I might patient be,*
*He sent me tribulation long and much,*
*It worked sweet patience as from self-will free*
*I yielded to His touch.*

*I asked the Lord that He my heart would fill*
*With His own fulness, and He emptied me*
*Of earthly things, of many treasures, till*
*My heart for Him was free.*

*I asked the Lord to make me keen in prayer,*
*He showed me all my great and mighty need*
*And that of others, which I sought to share -*
*Ah! then I prayed indeed.*

*I asked the Lord for Him I much might do,*
*To win Him many a soul 'twas this I sought;*
*He disciplined me, taught me, used me too,*
*Not just the way I thought.*

A.G. Fisher

## NOVEMBER — *Patience*

**1st**    I waited patiently for the Lord; and He inclined unto me, and heard my cry.

*Ps. 40:1*

**2nd**    Let us run with patience the race that is set before us, looking unto Jesus the author and finisher of our faith.

*Heb. 12:1-2*

**3rd**    Ye have need of patience, that, after ye have done the will of God, ye might receive the promise.

*Heb. 10:36*

**4th**    Tribulation worketh patience; and patience, experience; and experience, hope: and hope maketh not ashamed.

*Rom. 5:3-5*

**5th**    Sit still, my daughter, until thou know how the matter will fall.

*Ruth 3:18*

**6th**    Let patience have her perfect work, that ye may be perfect and entire, wanting nothing.

*James 1:4*

**7th**    The Lord direct your hearts into the love of God, and into the patient waiting for Christ.

*2 Thess 3:5*

## ❧ NOVEMBER ❧ *Grace*

**8th** By grace are ye saved through faith; and that not of yourselves: it is the gift of God.
*Eph. 2:8*

**9th** Where sin abounded, grace did much more abound.
*Rom. 5:20*

**10th** God resisteth the proud, but giveth grace unto the humble.
*James 4:6*

**11th** Let us have grace, whereby we may serve God acceptably with reverence and godly fear.
*Heb. 12:28*

**12th** My grace is sufficient for thee: for my strength is made perfect in weakness.
*2 Cor. 12:9*

**13th** It is a good thing that the heart be established with grace.
*Heb. 13:9*

**14th** God is able to make all grace abound toward you.
*2 Cor. 9:8*

## NOVEMBER — *Wisdom*

**15th** How much better is it to get wisdom than gold!
*Prov. 16:16*

**16th** The fear of the Lord is the beginning of wisdom.
*Ps. 111:10*

**17th** They that were foolish took their lamps, and took no oil with them.
*Matt. 25:3*

**18th** O that they were wise, that they understood this, that they would consider their latter end!
*Deut. 32:29*

**19th** They that were ready went in with Him to the marriage: and the door was shut.
*Matt. 25:10*

**20th** They that be wise shall shine as the brightness of the firmament.
*Daniel 12:3*

**21st** He that winneth souls is wise.
*Prov. 11:30*

# ☙ NOVEMBER ☙  *Strength*

**22<sup>nd</sup>** My flesh and my heart faileth: but God is the strength of my heart, and my portion for ever.

*Ps. 73:26*

**23<sup>rd</sup>** The Lord is the strength of my life; of whom shall I be afraid?

*Ps. 27:1*

**24<sup>th</sup>** The Lord is my rock, and my fortress, and my deliverer; my God, my strength.

*Ps. 18:2*

**25<sup>th</sup>** The Lord is my strength and my shield; my heart trusted in Him, and I am helped.

*Ps. 28:7*

**26<sup>th</sup>** Ye shall not go out with haste, nor go by flight: for the Lord will go before you.

*Isa. 52:12*

**27<sup>th</sup>** My grace is sufficient for thee; for my strength is made perfect in weakness.

*2 Cor. 12:9*

**28<sup>th</sup>** When I am weak then I am strong.

*2 Cor. 12:10*

**29<sup>th</sup>** Out of weakness ... made strong.

*Heb. 11:34*

**30<sup>th</sup>** To them that have no might He increaseth strength.

*Isa. 40:29*

# DECEMBER

## Henceforth Unto Him

To Thee, O Lord, do I lift up my soul,
Midst all the changes of this mortal life;
I long that Thou should'st each event control,
When days are calm, or when the storms are rife.

To Thee, the living God, my soul doth cry,
Thy tenderness and love inspire my trust;
I long to feel Thy presence ever nigh,
Most holy Father, gracious, true and just.

I fain would serve Thee, Lord, each day and hour,
No service is like Thine, so grand and free;
Let Thy blest Spirit come with quick'ning power
To bring new life and energy to me.

Just take me as I am, my God and King;
Work Thou through me Thy perfect, holy will;
To Thee my soul and body do I bring,
An "empty vessel" for Thy grace to fill.

Fanny Hope

# ❦ DECEMBER ❦        *Purity*

**1st**    Who can say, I have made may heart clean, I am pure from my sin?

*Prov. 20:9*

**2nd**    If we confess our sins, He is faithful and just to forgive ... and to cleanse.

*1 John 1:9*

**3rd**    Blessed are the pure in heart; for they shall see God.

*Matt. 5:8*

**4th**    Every man that hath this hope in Him purifieth himself, even as He is pure.

*1 John 3:3*

**5th**    See that ye love one another with a pure heart fervently.

*1 Peter 1:22*

**6th**    Be thou an example of the believers, in word, in conversation, in charity, in spirit, in faith, in purity.

*1 Tim. 4:12*

**7th**    A vessel unto honour, sanctified, and meet for the Master's use, and prepared unto every good work.

*2 Tim. 2:21*

## ☙ DECEMBER ☙

---

***8th***   Thou, which hast shewed me great and sore troubles, shalt quicken me again.
*Ps. 71:20*

***9th***   It is good for me that I have been afflicted; that I might learn Thy statutes.
*Ps. 119:71*

***10th***   In a great trial of affliction … their joy and their deep poverty abounded unto the riches of their liberality.
*2 Cor. 8:2*

***11th***   We went through fire and through water: but thou broughtest us out into a wealthy place.
*Ps. 66:12*

***12th***   Though I walk in the midst of trouble, Thou wilt revive me.
*Ps. 138:7*

***13th***   Though I walk through the valley of the shadow of death, I will fear no evil: for Thou art with me.
*Ps. 23:4*

***14th***   Our light affliction, which is but for a moment, worketh for us a far more exceeding and eternal weight of glory.
*2 Cor. 4:17*

## ❧ DECEMBER ❧           *Knowledge*

**15th**   YE KNOW that ye were not redeemed with corruptible things ... but with the precious blood of Christ.
*1 Peter 1:18-19*

**16th**   I count all things but loss for the excellency of the knowledge of Christ Jesus my Lord.
*Phil 3:8*

**17th**   The light of the knowledge of the glory of God in the face of Jesus Christ.
*2 Cor. 4:6*

**18th**   They took knowledge of them, that they had been with Jesus.
*Acts 4:13*

**19th**   WE KNOW that all things work together for good to them that love God.
*Rom. 8:28*

**20th**   WE KNOW that, when He shall appear, we shall be like Him.
*1 John 3:2*

**21st**   WE KNOW ... that we have a building of God, an house not made with hands, eternal in the heavens.
*2 Cor. 5:1*

## ≼ DECEMBER ≽ — *Following*

**22nd** Behold the Lamb of God! And the two disciples heard him speak, and they followed Jesus.

*John 1:36-37*

**23rd** Then shall we know, if we follow on to know the Lord.

*Hosea 6:3*

**24th** If any man serve Me, let him follow Me; and where I am there shall also My servant be.

*John 12:26*

**25th** The shepherds said one to another: Let us now go even unto Bethlehem.

*Luke 2:15*

**26th** Go and search diligently for the young Child.

*Matt. 2:8*

**27th** And lo, the star which they saw in the east went before them, till it came and stood over where the young Child was.

*Matt. 2:9*

**28th** He that followeth Me shall not walk in darkness, but shall have the light of life.

*John 8:12*

## ❧ DECEMBER ❧  *Following*

**29th** These are they which follow the Lamb whithersoever He goeth. These were redeemed from among men.
*Rev. 14:4*

**30th** His servants shall serve Him: and they shall see His face: and His name shall be in their foreheads.
*Rev. 22:3-4*

**31st** Forgetting those things which are behind, and reaching forth unto those things which are before, I press towards the mark for the prize of the high calling of God in Christ Jesus.
*Phil 3:13-14*